CW01151304

Sweet Treats

THE FINISHING TOUCH

Sweet Treats

AARON MAREE

CASSELL

To Angela Jarvis.

CASSELL
Villiers House
41-47 Strand
London WC2N 5JE

First published in the UK by Cassell 1993 by arrangement with
CollinsAngus&Robertson Publishers Pty Ltd

First published in Australia in 1993 by
CollinsAngus&Robertson Publishers Pty Limited
25 Ryde Road, Pymble NSW 2073 Australia

Copyright © Aaron Maree 1993

All rights reserved. No part of this publication may be reproduced or
transmitted in any form or by any means, electronic or mechanical
including photocopying, recording or any information storage or
retrieval system, without prior permission in writing from the publishers.

British Library Cataloguing-in-Publication data:
A catalogue record for this book is available from the British Library

ISBN 0 304 34255 6

Photographer: Andre Martin
Stylist: Karen Carter
Assistant Stylist: Katie Mitchell

Printed in the People's Republic of China

Contents

CHAPTER ONE - 7

Soft Sweets

CHAPTER TWO - 39

Hard Sweets

IMPORTANT NOTES - 61

ACKNOWLEDGEMENTS - 63

INDEX - 64

Chocolate Fudge

Chapter One

Soft Sweets

Sugar and sweets (candies) are among today's most popular and widely consumed foods. What makes sugar so appealing is its sweet taste and we humans have an innate liking for sweetness. Perhaps this comes from our early days as arboreal fruit-eaters. We have even incorporated sugar into our speech with terms like 'honey', 'sugar' and 'sweetheart' to describe our nearest and dearest. Somehow we must accept this sweet predicament of ours, revel in it instead and enjoy eating the delights of this book!

◆

Soft sweets are definitely a favourite as they are a popular treat to bring out for a special occasion or to eat at any time. Fudge, marzipan, marshmallow and nougat are all classic soft sweets which few can resist but most think are hard to create. This is not the case — anyone can make these timeless treats with ease and enjoyment.

Chocolate Fudge

2 cups (17 ½ oz) white granulated sugar
300 ml (10 ½ fl oz) thickened (double or heavy) cream
105 g (3 ½ oz) white compound chocolate
2 tablespoons (2 oz) liquid glucose (corn) syrup
15 g (½ oz) unsalted butter

Lightly oil or line with foil an 18 x 28 x 2 cm (7 x 11 x ¾ in) baking tray (sheet).

Place all ingredients into a large heavy-based saucepan and heat slowly while stirring with a wooden spoon. Bring the mixture to the boil and place a sugar (candy) thermometer (see p. 61) into the mixture, stirring continuously. Allow the mixture to boil until it reaches 118°C (245°F) or until it turns a light golden brown colour.

Remove the saucepan from the heat and continue stirring while the mixture cools.

When lukewarm beat the mixture vigorously until it loses its shine. Spread into the prepared tray. Flatten the mixture against the bottom of the tray then refrigerate until it is set. Cut into portions to serve.

Makes 30 medium portions

1. Boil the mixture until it reaches 118°C (245°F) or turns a light golden brown colour.

2. Beat the mixture vigorously until it loses its shine.

3. Spread the mixture into the prepared tray.

Fondant

3 cups (26 ½ oz) white granulated sugar
200 ml (7 fl oz) water
2 tablespoons (2 oz) liquid glucose (corn) syrup
cornflour (US cornstarch), for 'starch tray'

Place the ingredients into a heavy-based saucepan and bring slowly to the boil. Stir initially with a wooden spoon to ensure the sugar does not burn on the base of the pan. While the mixture is boiling, periodically wash down the sides of the saucepan with a pastry brush dipped in clean, warm water. When the mixture comes to the boil, insert a sugar (candy) thermometer (see p. 61) and continue boiling the mixture until it reaches 116°C (240°F). Remove the saucepan from the heat and sit it in a basin of cold water for a few seconds to stop the mixture from cooking.

Pour the syrup on to a marble slab and allow it to cool for a few minutes. With a wet palette knife turn the sides of the mixture into the centre so that the mix cools evenly. When the syrup has cooled and begun to thicken, work the mixture in a figure eight motion with a wooden spoon. Stir continuously until the mixture becomes very thick and white and crumbly. This process could take 5–8 minutes of stirring. Slightly moisten your hands with warm water and form the mixture into a ball. Wet your hands again if the mixture does not form easily.

Place the ball into a bowl and cover with a wet cloth. Leave in a cool place for 4–5 hours. When ready for use, place the bowl containing the fondant over a saucepan of boiling water and allow it to melt slowly over the steam. If the mix does not melt down add a tablespoon of water and allow the fondant to remain over the heat. Stir until a smooth paste forms. Do not allow the mix to heat beyond 35°C (95°F).

Note: Should the mixture not form a ball simply place the crumbly mix (and enough water to soften it) into a bowl over the boiling water and use immediately.

To Mould Fondants

One to two 'starch trays' are needed to mould individual fondants depending on their size. You make a 'starch tray' by sifting cornflour into the 25 x 30 x 3 cm (10 x 12 x 1 in) baking trays (sheets). Make sure the cornflour fills the trays to the top. Scrape a ruler across the top of the trays to level off the cornflour. Press the pointy end of an egg into the cornflour at regular intervals to make 18 round hollows in the cornflour. Do not make too many hollows as this will weaken the surface.

Pour the warm melted fondant into a piping (pastry) bag or simply spoon the fondant into each hollow and fill right to the top of each.

When all the hollows have been filled, lightly dust more cornflour over the top of each fondant. Place the tray in a cool dry place for 8 hours to allow the fondant to harden. Use a fork to carefully dig up each fondant. Use a fine pastry brush to remove the cornflour. Reserve and store the cornflour for future use. The fondants can be served as they are or dipped into chocolate and allowed to set before serving. Serve immediately or if covered with chocolate they can be stored in an airtight container for 3–4 days.

Makes 18

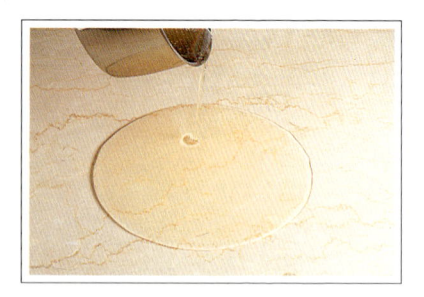

2. Pour the syrup on to a marble slab and allow to cool slightly.

3. Stir mix in a figure eight motion with a wooden spoon until it becomes thick and white.

1. Sit the saucepan of mixture in a basin of cold water for a few seconds to stop it from cooking.

4. Form the mixture into a ball with moistened hands.

SOFT SWEETS ~ 11

Fondant

Sweet Treats ~ 12

Walnut Toffee Fudge

Walnut Toffee Fudge

This confectionery should be deliciously smooth to the palate. Depending on the freshness of the walnuts they may require slight roasting to remove some of the oil which may cause the mixture to crystallise.

510 g (18 oz) unsalted butter
2 cups (18 oz) white granulated sugar
½ teaspoon lecithin granules
1 tablespoon (1 oz) liquid glucose (corn) syrup
1 cup (4 oz) walnuts, chopped

Grease well an 18 x 28 x 2 cm (7 x 11 x ¾ in) tray (sheet).

Melt the butter in a large heavy-based saucepan over medium heat. Add the granulated sugar and lecithin granules. Stir the mixture until it boils. Add the liquid glucose and continue to stir until the mixture reaches 150°C (302°F) on a sugar (candy) thermometer (see p. 61). Remove from the heat and stir in the walnuts. Pour into the prepared tray. When cool (do not cool in refrigerator) cut into squares before removing from the tray. Store in an airtight container in the refrigerator.

Makes 24–30

Coconut Ice

4 cups (35 oz) white granulated sugar
300 ml (10 ½ fl oz) milk
2 ½ tablespoons (2 ½ oz) liquid glucose (corn) syrup
2 ⅔ cups (9 oz) desiccated (shredded) coconut
2–3 drops pink food colouring

Lightly grease an 18 x 28 x 2 cm (7 x 11 x ¾ in) baking tray (sheet).
　Place the sugar, milk and glucose into a large, heavy-based saucepan. Stir over a low heat until the sugar is dissolved. Bring to the boil and continue to boil until the mixture reaches 112°C (235°F) on a sugar (candy) thermometer (see p. 61). Remove the saucepan from the heat and divide the mixture between two bowls. Add half of the coconut to each bowl. Stir the first mixture until it is thick and creamy and very white. Press it into the prepared tray. Colour the remaining mixture with the food colouring and beat until it is thick and creamy. Press on top of first mixture. When the combined mixture is cold and set, cut it into squares before removing from the tray. Store in an airtight container.

Makes 36

Chocolate Marzipan

½ cup (4 oz) caster (superfine) sugar
¾ cup (4 oz) icing (powdered) sugar, sifted
6 teaspoons (½ oz) cornflour (US cornstarch)
¼ cup (1 oz) cocoa powder
2 ¼ cups (8 ½ oz) ground almonds
1 egg, lightly beaten
375 g (13 oz) dark (plain or semi-sweet) chocolate, melted
2 cups (7 ½ oz) flaked almonds, roasted

Line a baking tray (sheet) with baking parchment. In a bowl mix together the caster sugar, icing sugar, cornflour, cocoa and ground almonds. Slowly add the egg and combine until the mixture forms a pliable dough. If the mixture seems a little dry add some more egg. If it feels a little moist, add more icing sugar to stiffen the dough. Cut the dough into four pieces and roll each piece into a sausage shape 1 cm (⅓ in) in diameter. Cut each sausage into twelve 3 cm (1 in) lengths. Dip each of these into the melted chocolate, then immediately roll them in the almonds. Place the pieces on to the prepared tray and place in the refrigerator until the chocolate has set. Serve with coffee or store in an airtight container.

Makes 48

SOFT SWEETS ~ 15

Chocolate Marzipan (above), Coconut Ice (below)

SWEET TREATS ~ 16

Marshmallow

Marshmallow

¼ cup (1 ½ oz) gelatine powder
180 ml (6 fl oz) cold water
3 cups (26 ½ oz) white granulated sugar
375 ml (13 fl oz) warm water
2 teaspoons lemon juice
1 teaspoon rose-water
desiccated (shredded) coconut, plain or toasted, for rolling

Sprinkle the gelatine over the cold water. Place the sugar and warm water into a saucepan over a gentle heat. Bring to the boil and add the soaked gelatine. Boil steadily for 20 minutes. Remove the saucepan from the heat and stir the mixture occasionally while it becomes lukewarm. Pour the liquid into a mixing bowl and add the lemon juice and rose-water. Whisk until it becomes pure white and triples in volume. Pour the whisked marshmallow into an 18 x 28 x 2 cm (7 x 11 x ¾ in) tray. Alternatively it can be poured into shaped moulds like a starch tray (see p. 9) or piped into shapes. Refrigerate overnight. Remove the marshmallow from the refrigerator and, using a sharp hot knife, cut it into small squares. Roll each square in the plain or toasted coconut. Store in an airtight container.
Note: To remove the marshmallows from moulding containers (but not the starch tray) the bottom of the containers may need to be quickly dipped into warm water.

Makes 30–36

Sugared Jellies

250 ml (9 fl oz) clear apple juice
2 tablespoons (1 oz) gelatine powder
15 ml (½ fl oz) Calvados (apple brandy)
1 ½ cups (12 ½ oz) caster (superfine) sugar
¼ cup (2 ½ oz) clear honey
white granulated sugar, for rolling

Place half the apple juice into a small bowl and sprinkle the powdered gelatine over it. Allow to soak for 30 minutes.

Place the remaining juice, Calvados, sugar and honey into a saucepan. Slowly bring this mixture to the boil. Add the soaked gelatine to the boiling liquid and stir until completely dissolved. Allow the liquid to boil until it reaches 112°C (233°F) on a sugar (candy) thermometer (p. 61). Pour the mixture into an 18 x 28 x 2 cm (7 x 11 x ¾ in) baking tray (sheet) and allow to cool before placing in the refrigerator for 48 hours.

When firm cut the jelly into small oblong-shaped pieces with a knife dipped in hot water and roll each piece in granulated sugar. Serve the jellies immediately. Do not sugar coat any pieces which are not to be served immediately. Store them in an airtight container in a cool place.

Makes 40

SOFT SWEETS ~ 19

Sugared Jellies

Sweet Treats ~ 20

Coconut Kisses

Coconut Kisses

1 ¼ cups (7 ½ oz) icing (powdered) sugar, sifted
60 g (2 oz) unsalted butter, softened
2 tablespoons hot water
1 cup (3 ½ oz) desiccated (shredded) coconut
300 g (10 ½ oz) dark (plain or semi-sweet) chocolate, melted

Line a baking tray (sheet) with baking parchment.

Place the icing sugar, butter and hot water into a bowl and mix together until completely combined. Place the bowl over a saucepan of boiling water and beat for 8–10 minutes or until the mixture is quite warm and very liquid. Add the coconut and stir together.

Working quickly, use two teaspoons to form the mixture into oval shapes. As each oval is shaped, place it carefully on the prepared tray. Place the tray in the refrigerator for 1 hour so the kisses can harden.

Remove the tray from the refrigerator. Melt the chocolate and dip each Coconut Kiss into the chocolate. Alternatively, drizzle the chocolate over the top. Place back into the refrigerator to set the chocolate. Store in an airtight container in the refrigerator.

Makes 24–30

Nougat

2 ⅓ cups (22 oz) white granulated sugar
1 cup (10 oz) liquid glucose (corn) syrup
⅓ cup (4 oz) clear honey
2 egg whites
¾ cup (3 oz) flaked almonds
½ cup (2 oz) hazelnuts, chopped
½ cup (3 ½ oz) glacé (candied) pineapple, chopped

Preheat oven to 200°C (390°F). Line an 18 x 28 x 2 cm (7 x 11 x ¾ in) baking tray (sheet) with baking parchment.

Place the sugar, glucose and honey into a large heavy-based saucepan and bring slowly to the boil. Whilst boiling stir the mixture to ensure that the sugar does not burn on the sides of the saucepan. (Do not worry about dissolving the sugar prior to boiling. Simply mix so that the ingredients combine.) Place a sugar (candy) thermometer (see p. 61) into the mixture and boil to 140°C (284°F).

Place the egg whites into the mixing bowl of a powerful electric mixer and whisk on a medium speed until they form stiff peaks. As the egg whites are being whipped, begin drizzling the boiled mixture into the whites. Mix until all the boiled mixture is combined. The combined mixture should be very thick and stiff. Place the almonds and chopped hazelnuts on to an unlined baking tray (sheet) and place into the preheated oven for 8 minutes.

Fold the hot nuts and pineapple through the egg white mixture with a wooden spoon. Spoon the nougat mixture into the prepared tray. Place more baking parchment over the top. Make the mix flat and even by firmly pressing down the baking parchment. Allow the Nougat to sit in a cool place for 6 hours (or overnight) to firm and set.

Cut the Nougat into finger-sized slices with a lightly oiled knife before serving. Wrap each piece of Nougat in cellophane and store in an airtight container.

Makes 36–40

Nougat

Walnut Logs

1 cup (8 oz) caster (superfine) sugar
2 ½ tablespoons (2 ½ oz) golden (dark corn) syrup
120 g (4 oz) unsalted butter
⅓ cup (4 oz) liquid glucose (corn) syrup
390 g (13 oz) sweetened condensed milk
1 tablespoon instant coffee granules dissolved in 85 ml (3 fl oz) hot water
2 ½ cups (10 ½ oz) walnuts, chopped
360 g (12 ½ oz) dark (plain or semi-sweet) chocolate, melted

Lightly grease an 18 x 28 x 2 cm (7 x 11 x ¾ in) baking tray (sheet).

Place the sugar, golden syrup, butter, glucose and condensed milk into a large heavy-based saucepan. Stir continuously and slowly allow the mixture to come to the boil. Continue boiling the mixture until it becomes thick and a light golden brown colour. Keep stirring the mixture at all times as it will stick to the saucepan and burn very quickly. Add the coffee mixture. Remove the saucepan from the heat and pour the mixture into the prepared tray. Refrigerate until firm (overnight if possible).

When firm, cut into 6 strips, cutting across the breadth of the baking tray. Remove the strips from the tray and quickly roll them into round logs on a clean surface. Once rounded, roll the logs in the chopped walnuts to completely coat them. Place the walnut-covered logs on to a flat tray and freeze for 30 minutes.

Pour the melted chocolate into a 18 x 28 x 2 cm (7 x 11 x ¾ in) baking tray (sheet). Remove the logs from the freezer and place them into the chocolate one at a time. Roll them so that they are completely covered. Once covered, remove the chocolate logs to a flat baking tray (sheet), lined with baking parchment and allow to stand until the chocolate has set firm. If required immediately, simply cut the logs into slices using a hot knife. If being stored, wrap each log individually in plastic (cling) wrap and refrigerate until required.

Makes six 18 cm (7 in) logs (each cut into 12 pieces)

1. When firm, cut the mixture into strips across the breadth of the baking tray.

SOFT SWEETS ~ 25

Walnut Logs

SWEET TREATS ~ 26

2. Roll the logs of chilled mix in the chopped walnuts.

3. Roll the logs in chocolate.

Walnut Marzipan

1 ¾ cups (14 oz) white granulated sugar
2 tablespoons (2 oz) liquid glucose (corn) syrup
100 ml (3 ½ fl oz) water
1 ⅓ cups (5 oz) ground almonds
1 ⅔ cups (7 oz) ground walnuts
cornflour (US cornstarch), for dusting
360 g (12 ½ oz) dark (plain or semi-sweet) chocolate, melted
24–30 walnut halves, for decoration

Lightly dust an 18 x 28 x 2 cm (7 x 11 x ¾ in) baking tray (sheet) with cornflour.

Place the sugar, glucose and water into a saucepan and stir over a low heat using a wooden spoon. Stir until the sugar has dissolved. Increase the heat and allow the mixture to come to the boil. Boil the mixture until it reaches 116°C (240°F) on a sugar (candy) thermometer.

Place the almonds and walnuts into a mixing bowl, add the boiled liquid and combine. Do not overmix. Remove the mixture from the bowl and place it on the prepared tray. Quickly dust the mixture lightly with cornflour and roll it to 1 cm (⅓ in) thickness. (The mixture may seem soft to start with but it will start to harden very quickly once rolled.) Using a 2–3 cm (¾–1 in) plain round cookie cutter dipped in cornflour, quickly cut out pieces from the rolled mix. Dip each piece into the melted dark chocolate and place a walnut half on top of each. Set the pieces on a tray and allow the chocolate to harden before serving with coffee. Store in an airtight container.

Makes 24–30

1. Add the boiled liquid to the dry mixture.

2. Quickly dust with cornflour and roll the mixture to 1 cm (⅓ in) thickness.

SWEET TREATS ~ 28

3. Using a plain round cookie cutter, cut out pieces of mixture.

4. Dip each piece into the melted dark chocolate and place half a walnut on top of each.

SOFT SWEETS ~ 29

Walnut Marzipan

Turkish Delight

Turkish Delight

Invented centuries ago in the Middle East, this gelatinous, sweet confection is usually dusted in either cornflour (US cornstarch) or icing (powdered) sugar or both. Flavours can change according to recipes but Turkish Delight is traditionally made either red or clear and flavoured with rose-water or citrus rinds.

2 cups (17 ½ oz) white granulated sugar
250 ml (9 fl oz) water mixed with 1 or 2 drops of rose-water
grated rind of one orange
⅔ cup (3 oz) cornflour (US cornstarch)
120 ml (4 fl oz) orange juice
2 tablespoons (1 oz) gelatine powder, soaked in 3 tablespoons cold water
2–3 drops red (cochineal) food colouring
½ cup (3 oz) icing (powdered) sugar, for dusting
⅔ cup (3 oz) cornflour (US cornstarch), for dusting

Lightly oil an 18 x 28 x 2 cm (7 x 11 x ¾ in) baking tray (sheet).

Place the sugar, water and orange rind in a large saucepan over a gentle heat. Stir until the sugar has dissolved, then increase heat and bring to the boil. Add the first amount of cornflour to the orange juice and mix to a paste. Quickly whisk the paste into the boiling liquid and allow the mixture to come to the boil again. Add the soaked gelatine and stir to ensure all ingredients are well combined. Add the red food colouring. Boil the mixture for 10 minutes, stirring continuously to ensure the mix does not burn. Pour the mixture through a fine sieve into the prepared tray. Refrigerate for 12–24 hours before cutting into squares with a hot sharp knife. Mix the second amount of cornflour and icing sugar together and sift to ensure they are evenly mixed. Drop the squares of Turkish Delight into the powdery mix and coat each piece well. Serve immediately or store in an airtight container in the refrigerator.

Note: The firmness or jelly-like consistency of this sweet can be varied by using more or less cornflour or gelatine.

Makes 36–40

Rum Balls

1 ⅔ cups (7 ½ oz) sponge cakecrumbs
3 tablespoons chocolate drinking powder
1 tablespoon cocoa powder
1 cup (3 oz) desiccated (shredded) coconut
¾ cup (3 oz) flaked almonds, roasted
3 tablespoons rum (brown (dark) or white (light))
30 g (1 oz) unsalted butter
2 tablespoons (2 oz) apricot jam
375 g (13 oz) dark (plain or semi-sweet) chocolate, melted
240 g (8 ½ oz) milk chocolate, coarsely grated
¾ cup (4 oz) icing (powdered) sugar, for dusting

Place the sponge cake crumbs, chocolate drinking powder, cocoa, coconut, almonds, rum, butter and apricot jam into a bowl and mix together by hand until they are combined. (Depending on the moisture of the sponge, add more alcohol if it is too dry or add coconut if it is too moist.) Take a heaped tablespoon of the mixture, roll into a ball and place on a tray (sheet). Repeat until all the mixture is used. Place the tray in the refrigerator for 5 minutes.

Place the melted dark chocolate and grated milk chocolate in separate bowls ready for use. Roll each of the balls by hand in the melted chocolate and then place directly into the grated chocolate. It is a good idea to have a second person roll the balls to ensure an even covering. Finally, dust each ball with icing sugar.

Makes 36–40

SOFT SWEETS ~ 33

Rum Balls

Apricot Delights

3 cups (7 ½ oz) dried apricots
2 x 500 ml (17 ½ fl oz) boiling water
60 g (2 oz) unsalted butter, softened
⅓ cup (2 oz) icing (powdered) sugar
2 cups (6 oz) desiccated (shredded) coconut
grated rind 1 orange
melted dark (plain or semi-sweet) chocolate, for dipping (optional)

Place the dried apricots into a large bowl and pour over 500 ml (17 ½ fl oz) of boiling water. Allow the apricots to sit for 2 hours. Drain the apricots and pour another 500 ml (17 ½ fl oz) of boiling water over them and allow them to sit for another 2 hours. Drain the apricots and place them into a mixing bowl with the butter, icing sugar, coconut and orange rind. Mix until the ingredients are well combined. Remove the mixture from the bowl and press into an 18 x 28 x 2 cm (7 x 11 x ¾ in) baking tray (sheet) and refrigerate for 12 hours. Cut the mixture into squares. Dip into chocolate or leave plain.

Makes 36–40

SOFT SWEETS ~ 35

Apricot Delights

SWEET TREATS ~ 36

Candied (Crystallised) Fruit

Candied (Crystallised) Fruit

Candied fruit is used for decorating cakes or petits fours or can be eaten on its own. This recipe must be prepared well in advance.

750 g (26 ½ oz) fresh fruit (oranges, lemons, pineapples, or grapefruit)
500 ml (17 ½ fl oz) water
1 ⅔ cups (10 ½ oz) white granulated sugar
½ cup (6 oz) liquid glucose (corn) syrup

Peel the fruit and cut into fine slices ready for boiling. Place the water into a saucepan and bring to the boil. Place the sliced fruit into the boiling water for 1 minute before removing and allowing to cool on a wire cooling rack. Retain the water. Place the sugar and glucose into the reserved water and bring to the boil. Place the cooled cooked fruit into a glass or ceramic casserole dish. Pour the boiling liquid over the top of the fruit. Leave the mixture for 24 hours.

Drain the liquid from the fruit. Place the liquid into a saucepan and bring to the boil. Pour the boiled liquid over the fruit and leave for 24 hours.

Repeat this process for the next 3 days, simply draining the fruit, boiling the liquid and pouring it back over the fruit. After 3 days, the fruit may remain in the syrup to be used as soft crystallised fruit, or can be removed from the liquid, drained on a wire cooling rack and allowed to dry. Use the fruit immediately or if storing, put it in an airtight container in the refrigerator for 1–2 weeks.

Makes approximately 1 cup (10 oz)

Butterscotch (above), Lollipops (left), Caramels (right), Peanut Brittle (below).

Chapter Two

Hard Sweets

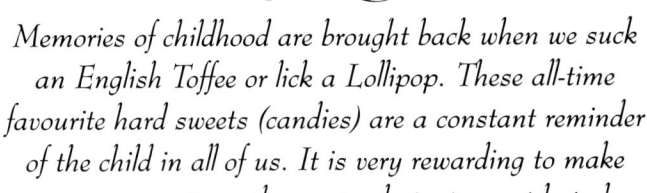

Memories of childhood are brought back when we suck an English Toffee or lick a Lollipop. These all-time favourite hard sweets (candies) are a constant reminder of the child in all of us. It is very rewarding to make your own sweets as they not only taste great but also look colourful and festive in jars around the kitchen.

◆

There are a few safety measures you must follow when making hard sweets but if you are cautious when dealing with hot sugar syrup confectionery you should enjoy the creation and consumption of these heavenly delights.

Boiled Sweets (Candies)

Boiled Sweets are perhaps the most difficult confectionery to create due to the extreme temperature of the syrup that must be formed with your hands (see p. 61). If it is produced correctly it should be quite hot yet easy to stretch. When producing this kind of confectionery you should always work on a marble slab which is lightly oiled.

2 cups (17 ½ oz) white granulated sugar
250 ml (9 fl oz) water
¼ cup (3 ½ oz) liquid glucose (corn) syrup
5 drops of tartaric acid

Place the sugar and water into a large heavy-based saucepan and dissolve slowly over a gentle heat. When the sugar is completely dissolved, allow the mixture to come to the boil. As the mixture boils, wash down the sides of the saucepan with a pastry brush dipped in warm water to remove any mixture that has splashed up the sides of the pan. Add the glucose to the mixture and stir in using a clean spoon. Continue cleaning the sides of the saucepan and allow the syrup to return to the boil. Remove the saucepan from the heat and pour the syrup directly into a large jar that has a tight-fitting lid. Store the syrup in the container for 12–24 hours. Storing the syrup in this way helps all the sugar crystals to dissolve.

Pour the syrup into a clean saucepan and bring it to the boil. Be sure once again to wash down the sides of the saucepan. Place a sugar (candy) thermometer (see p. 61) into the boiling liquid. Once it has reached 120°C (250°F) there is no need to continue washing down the sides of the saucepan. Allow the mixture to reach 137°C (280°F) on the sugar thermometer and add the tartaric acid. Continue boiling the mixture until it reaches 154°C (310°F).

Remove the sugar thermometer carefully, then pour syrup on to a lightly oiled marble slab. Allow it to cool for several minutes until a slight skin forms. Using a lightly oiled metal scraper, scrape the outer edges of the syrup into the centre. Allow it to spread out again before scraping the outer edges into the middle once more. Repeat this process until the syrup becomes fairly cool and forms a firm ball. The syrup should still feel fairly hot to touch, but should not burn.

With lightly oiled hands and a scraper, pull the syrup into a long sausage shape. Take each end of the sausage shape and stretch it to triple its original length. Fold the ends of the sausage shape together and stretch it again. Fold the two ends back together and repeat the process

HARD SWEETS ~ 41

Boiled Sweets (Candies)

several times until the mixture changes from a clear to silky white colour. This should take 10–15 minutes. When the sausage shape reaches this colour, pull it one last time, and a little longer than usual. Fold it in half and then in half again and twist each length around and around so that it forms a long fine rope.

Using lightly oiled scissors, cut this rope into 1 cm (⅓ in) lengths and allow the sweets to cool on the oiled marble until they are firm. Store the sweets in an airtight jar.
Note: Should the syrup crystallise or harden before it becomes a silky white colour, all you need to do is, place it into a saucepan with ½ cup water and slowly mix until the hard sugar has dissolved. Boil the mixture to 155°C (310°F) and repeat the whole process.

Makes 50

1. Pour the boiled mixture on to a lightly oiled marble slab.

2. As the syrup cools slightly, use a lightly oiled metal scraper to scrape the cold outer edges into the centre of the syrup.

3. When syrup has cooled pull it into a long sausage shape.

4. Fold, twist and pull the sausage shape.

HARD SWEETS ~ 43

5. Continue this process until the sausage shape becomes silky white in colour.

6. Using lightly oiled scissors, cut the rope into 1 cm ($\frac{1}{3}$ in) lengths.

SWEET TREATS ~ 44

English Toffee

English Toffee

2 cups (18 oz) white granulated sugar
85 ml (3 fl oz) water
⅔ cup (8 ½ oz) golden
(dark corn) syrup
240 g (8 ½ oz) unsalted butter
2 tablespoons (2 oz) liquid glucose
(corn) syrup

Lightly oil an 18 x 28 x 2 cm (7 x 11 x ¾ in) baking tray (sheet).

Place the sugar, water and golden syrup into a saucepan and dissolve slowly over a gentle heat. Bring the mixture to the boil. Add the butter and glucose; allow the mix to continue to boil while you keep stirring it. Insert a sugar (candy) thermometer (see p. 61) and boil to 135°C (275°F). Pour the boiled mixture immediately into the prepared tray and allow to cool.

When the toffee is almost set use a lightly oiled knife to mark it into small squares. Marking the mixture enables it to be broken into uniform pieces when hard. Allow to cool completely, before placing in the refrigerator for 2 hours to set solid. Once solid remove carefully from the tray and break into the marked portions. Wrap each portion in cellophane wrapping and place in an airtight container. Store in the refrigerator until required.

Makes 40–50

Caramels

◆

2 cups (17 ½ oz) white granulated sugar
1 ½ cups (9 oz) soft (light) brown sugar
250 ml (9 fl oz) water
60 ml (2 fl oz) white wine vinegar

Place all ingredients into a large saucepan and slowly bring to the boil. Wash down the sides of the saucepan using a pastry brush dipped in warm water. Place a sugar (candy) thermometer (see p. 61) into the boiling liquid and boil the mixture to 145°C (295°F). Remove from the heat and place the basin of the saucepan into a basin of cold water to stop the caramel from cooking. Using a ladle, pour small amounts of caramel into paper patty cake cases which have been placed in a muffin tray (patty pan) so they hold their shape. Half fill each paper case then allow the caramel to cool and harden before serving. Store in an airtight container in the refrigerator.

Makes 24

Honeycomb

◆

1 ½ cups (13 ½ oz) white granulated sugar
⅓ cup (4 ½ oz) clear honey
1 tablespoon (1 oz) liquid glucose (corn) syrup
¼ cup (3 oz) golden (dark corn) syrup
85 ml (3 fl oz) water
2 teaspoons bicarbonate of soda (baking soda)

Grease an 25 x 30 x 3 cm (10 x 12 x 1 in) baking tray (sheet).

Combine the sugar, honey, glucose, golden syrup and water in a large heavy-based saucepan. Stir over a gentle heat until all the ingredients dissolve. Bring the mixture to the boil and continue boiling until it reaches 132°C (270°F) on a sugar (candy) thermometer (see p. 61). When this temperature has been reached, remove the sugar thermometer and reduce the heat so the mixture simmers. Continue simmering for a further 15 minutes. Remove the saucepan from the heat and allow the bubbles to subside. Sift the bicarbonate of soda to ensure it has no lumps. Using a wooden spoon, stir in the soda and allow the mixture to become frothy. Pour it immediately into the prepared tray and allow it to cool before breaking into bite-size pieces.

Makes 30 portions

HARD SWEETS ~ 47

Honeycomb (above), Caramels (below)

Toffee Apples

2 cups (17 ½ oz) white granulated sugar
250 ml (9 fl oz) water
¼ cup (3 ½ oz) liquid glucose (corn) syrup
2–3 drops of red (cochineal) or green food colouring
6 large, firm, flavoursome green apples

Place the sugar and water into a large heavy-based saucepan and dissolve very slowly over a gentle heat. When the sugar is completely dissolved, allow the mixture to come to the boil. As the mixture boils wash down the sides of the saucepan with a pastry brush dipped in warm water to remove any mixture that has splashed or boiled up the sides. Add the glucose to the boiling mixture and stir in using a clean metal spoon. Once again wash down the sides of the saucepan with a wet pastry brush and allow the mixture to return to the boil. Remove the saucepan from the heat and pour the syrup directly into a large jar that has a tight-fitting lid. Storing the syrup in this way helps all the sugar crystals to dissolve. Store the syrup in the container for 12–24 hours.

Line a baking tray (sheet) with baking parchment.

Pour the syrup into a clean saucepan and bring the mixture to the boil. Be sure once again to wash down the sides of the saucepan with a pastry brush dipped in warm water. Place a sugar (candy) thermometer (see p. 61) into the boiling liquid. Once it has reached 120°C (250°F) there is no need to continue washing down the sides of the saucepan. When the mixture reaches 125°C (260°F), add drops of the food colouring. Continue boiling the mixture until it reaches 155°C (310°F). Remove the sugar thermometer carefully, then allow the bubbles to subside and let the mixture cool slightly.

Wash and carefully dry the apples. Press large wooden skewers into the bottom end of each apple and push them halfway into the apple. Hold the skewer with the apple attached and dip it into the sugar, swirling it around so that the apple is well coated. Remove the apple and allow the excess toffee to drip off. Place the apples on to the prepared tray. Repeat this process with each apple. Leave the apples on the tray until they have cooled and the sugar has set. Wrap each apple in plastic (cling) wrap or coloured cellophane as soon as it hardens.

Note: Depending on the humidity in which you are working, these childhood favourites can last from 1 to 5 days. Keep them wrapped to prolong their life and also for effective presentation and sale.

Makes 6

HARD SWEETS ~ 49

Toffee Apples

SWEET TREATS ~ 50

Peanut Brittle

Peanut Brittle

250 ml (9 fl oz) water
2 cups (17 ½ oz) white granulated sugar
30 g (1 oz) unsalted butter
1 ¾ cups (9 ½ oz) dry roasted peanuts
240 g (8 ½ oz) dark (plain or semi-sweet) chocolate, melted

Lightly oil an 18 x 28 x 2 cm (7 x 11 x ¾ in) baking tray (sheet) and line it with foil.

Place the water and sugar into a large heavy-based saucepan and slowly bring to the boil. Stir the mixture only to move the sugar around and prevent it from burning on the base of the saucepan. Place a sugar (candy) thermometer (see p. 61) into the mixture and allow it to boil to 150°C (300°F). While the mixture reaches this temperature, periodically wash down the sides of the saucepan with a pastry brush dipped in warm water. This will remove any stray sugar crystals. When the mixture reaches 150°C (300°F) remove the sugar thermometer and add the butter. Stir the mixture with a long-handled wooden spoon until all the butter is dissolved and incorporated. Add the peanuts quickly and stir until combined. Pour the mixture into the prepared tray. Spread the peanut mixture as smoothly and evenly as possible in the tray. Allow the mixture to cool at room temperature until hard and cold.

Spread the top of the Peanut Brittle with half of the melted chocolate and place it in the refrigerator for 2–3 minutes until the chocolate is firm enough to handle. Turn the mixture out of the tray on to another baking tray. Peel away the foil from the base of the brittle. Wipe away any excess oil and then cover the base with the remaining half of the chocolate. Allow this to set in the refrigerator for 3–4 minutes, then remove immediately. Break the brittle into bite-size pieces and store in an airtight jar at room temperature until required. Store for only short periods of time, especially in humid conditions, and serve fresh if possible.

Makes 30 medium-sized pieces

Lollipops

2 cups (17 ½ oz) white granulated sugar
250 ml (9 fl oz) water
¼ cup (3 ½ oz) liquid glucose (corn) syrup
3–4 drops of red (cochineal) food colouring

Place the sugar and water into a large heavy-based saucepan and dissolve slowly over a gentle heat. When the sugar is completely dissolved, allow the mixture to come to the boil. As the mixture boils wash down the sides of the saucepan with a pastry brush dipped in warm water to remove any mix that has splashed or boiled up the sides of the pan. Add the glucose to the boiling mixture and stir in using a clean metal spoon. Continue washing down the sides of the saucepan and allow the mixture to return to the boil. Remove the saucepan from the heat and pour the syrup into a large jar that has a tight-fitting lid. Storing the syrup in this way helps all the sugar crystals to dissolve. Store the syrup in the container for 12–24 hours.

Pour the syrup into a clean saucepan and bring the mixture to the boil. Be sure once again to wash down the sides of the saucepan with a pastry brush dipped in warm water. Place a sugar (candy) thermometer (see p. 61) into the boiling liquid. Once it has reached 120°C (250°F) there is no need to continue washing down the sides of the saucepan.

Allow the mixture to reach 125°C (260°F) and add the red food colouring. Continue to boil the mixture until it reaches 155°C (310°F). Carefully remove the sugar thermometer. Using a tablespoon, spoon small amounts of the mixture on to a lightly oiled marble slab or on to baking parchment. Allow the syrup to cool for several minutes until a slight skin forms. Press a toothpick or lollipop stick into each round of mixture. Wrap in cellophane and store in an airtight container.

Makes 24

HARD SWEETS ~ 53

Lollipops

Sugar Bells

Sugar Bells

Used mainly for the decoration of anniversary, birthday, wedding and special-occasion cakes, these delights can also be made into petits fours if made very thinly. Use them instead of place-cards at the dining table. Your guests can eat the bells with their after-dinner coffee.

*1 tablespoon egg white
approximately 2 cups (17 oz) white granulated sugar*

Place the egg white into a mixing bowl and use a spoon to mix in half the sugar. Continue adding sugar until the mixture has the consistency of moist sand. Do not make the mixture too dry as it will not hold together. Do not make it too wet either as it may dissolve. Using a teaspoon, press the sugar mixture into a bell-shaped mould. After each teaspoon of mixture is added, press it in firmly with your fingers. Continue adding the mixture until the mould is full. Place the bell upside down on a sheet of baking parchment and tap the mould using the spoon. The sugar bell should drop from the mould on to the paper. Leave uncovered for 3–4 hours.

Very carefully pick the bell up and, using a small knife, cut away the inside sugar so you only leave a fine outside crust. Smooth the inside of the bell with your fingers and place it back on the paper. Leave overnight to firm. You can pipe decorations or names on to the sides of the bells with a fine paper piping bag filled with Royal Icing (see p. 62) or melted chocolate.

Makes approximately 3–4 bells

1. Press the sugar mixture into the bell-shaped mould until the mould is full.

2. Very carefully use a small knife to cut away the inside of the sugar so that you only leave a fine outside crust.

Praline

◆

Praline, also known as Croquant, is a mixture of caramelised sugar and almonds. Traditionally used as a flavouring for ganaches or creams in its crushed form, this mixture can also be enjoyed today as a treat on its own and as a cake decoration.

1 ¼ cups (10 ½ oz) white granulated sugar
2 ¼ cups (9 oz) flaked almonds

Heat a heavy-based saucepan over medium heat. Slowly sprinkle the sugar into the pan and allow to melt before adding more. Keep slowly adding the sugar and continue to stir. Heat until all the sugar has melted and is a dark golden brown. Immediately stir in the flaked almonds.

To make individual treats, take tablespoons of the mix and place on to a baking tray (sheet) lined with baking parchment. When the tray is full allow the pieces to set and cool at room temperature before serving.

To make a cake decoration for a rectangular cake, lightly oil a baking tray (sheet) which is the same size as the cake you are decorating and line it with foil. Pour the hot mixture into the prepared tray and spread it so that it neatly covers the entire surface. Roll an oiled rolling pin gently over the top of the mix to flatten it. Allow the mixture to sit for several minutes until it firms slightly. Remove the mixture from the tray. Peel the foil from the back of the mixture. Peel one corner of the praline back and allow it to set over a lightly oiled cylindrical object or small rolling pin. Allow the mixture to cool in this position. When hard remove the cylinder and decorate the praline sheet with piped melted white chocolate or Royal Icing (see p. 62) before placing it on top of a cake.

To make a decoration for a round cake, lightly oil the surface of a flat metal or marble bench (counter) top and place a round cake or tartlet ring on to the surface. Pour the hot praline mixture into the centre of the ring and spread out using an oiled spoon. Make sure the praline covers the area evenly and smoothly. Allow to cool slightly and remove the ring.

Slide a sharp knife or scraper carefully under the cooling disc to loosen it. Use a lightly oiled pizza cutting wheel or a large sharp knife to mark the disc into 8 portions. Make sure these marks are 2 cm (¾ in) from the edge. Once marked, carefully cut the portions through carefully, making sure the 2 cm (¾ in) outer ring is not cut or broken. Fold the cuts from the centre towards the outer edge to form a crown. Place a bowl or small dish in the centre to support the folded-back portions. Remove the bowl when the praline hardens and decorate with piped

Praline

melted white chocolate or Royal Icing (see p. 62) or leave plain. Place the decoration on top of a round cake to serve.

1. To make a rectangular cake decoration, pour the sugar and almond mixture into the prepared tray.

2. When the Praline has firmed for the rectangular decoration, carefully peel back one corner and allow it to set over a cylindrical object.

3. To make a round cake decoration, use a lightly oiled knife or pizza wheel to cut the cooled disc into wedges, staying 2 cm (¾ in) from the edge.

4. Peel back each wedge to form a crown.

Butterscotch

120 ml (4 fl oz) water
3 cups (26 ½ oz) white granulated sugar
¾ cup (11 ½ oz) liquid glucose (corn) syrup
180 g (6 oz) unsalted butter

Grease an 18 x 28 x 2 cm (7 x 11 x ¾ in) baking tray (sheet).

Combine the water, sugar and glucose in a large saucepan and stir over a low heat until the sugar has dissolved. While the mixture is boiling, brush down the sides of the saucepan with a pastry brush dipped in warm water. This should clean any splashes or granules of sugar. When the mixture has come to the boil, place a sugar (candy) thermometer into the pan and allow the mix to boil to 150°C (302°F). When it has reached this temperature the mixture should be a pale amber colour.

Remove the pan from the heat and allow the bubbles to subside before adding the butter. Stir the butter into the mixture with a long-handled wooden spoon, taking care not to splash yourself with the hot mixture. Continue to stir until the butter is combined. Pour the stirred mixture into the prepared tray and allow to cool slightly before scoring the top with a lightly oiled knife. Once cold, break the Butterscotch into the marked pieces.

Makes 48

Butterscotch

Important Notes

All ingredients should be at room temperature when used unless the recipe advises otherwise. Ensure that all utensils are clean, dry and grease free before cooking. Water or grease on utensils can adversely affect recipes, especially when using egg whites, which will not reach maximum aeration if mixed with even small amounts of grease or water.

Egg Weights

All eggs used in these recipes should be 55–60 g (approximately 2 oz).

Baking Tray (Sheet) Sizes

In all the recipes we have endeavoured to provide you with international tray sizes but if you find that the tray size suggested is not available please use the closest size you can find. For this reason you may need two trays when we suggest one.

Cooking with Sugar

Confectionery must be boiled at an extremely high temperature and so can be very dangerous. Please use extreme caution when creating confectionery as sugar at this temperature will stick to your skin and burn.

During the pulling of sweets your hands will come into contact with the hot sugar. If your hands become too hot, place them flat on a clean cool area of your marble slab for several seconds. If you find that you simply cannot pick up the sugar long enough to pull it you may have crystallised the sugar and will have to start again. If the sugar eventually becomes cooler as you pull it you have produced it correctly.

Sugar (Candy) Thermometer

To care for your thermometer, always wash it well after use. Before placing the thermometer in a boiling mixture, sit it in a saucepan of hot water and when you remove it from a boiling mixture, return it to the hot water. This reduces the shock of the change in temperatures and decreases the chance of the liquid in the thermometer forming air bubbles.

Storage of Confectionery

Do not store confectionery for extended periods of time unless otherwise advised in the recipe. Moisture and humidity will begin to soften and dissolve confectionery and varying temperatures can crystallise it. Recommended shelf life is approximately 3–4 days in most cases. Do not refrigerate confectionery unless advised to do so as this can cause condensation which will dissolve the confectionery.

Royal Icing

3 cups (17 oz) icing (powdered) sugar, sifted
2 egg whites
½ teaspoon lemon juice

Mix the egg whites with the icing sugar until well combined. Beat the mixture until it forms stiff peaks. Add the lemon juice and mix in. If the mixture is too stiff to pipe through a piping (pastry) bag, add a small amount of extra egg white. If it is too wet add extra icing sugar a tablespoon at a time. Keep the icing covered with a damp cloth when storing for a few hours to prevent it from crusting and going hard. If you are storing the icing for a few days place it in a plastic bag inside a plastic container. Do not store it for more than 3 days and beat for 5–10 minutes before re-using.

OVEN TEMPERATURES AND GAS MARKS

DEGREES (F)	200	225	250	275	300	325	350	375	400	425	450
GAS MARK 1	¼	½	1	2	3	4	5	6	7	8	9
GAS MARK 2	1	2	3	4	5	6	7	8	9	10	11

Acknowledgements

The author would like to thank the following people and organisations for their assistance and support:

Gwen Gedeon, from The Welsh Lady Patisserie, for her professional generosity

Brian Cox, General Manager, Socomin International Fine Foods, for their Odense range of products

Paul Frizzel, Account Executive, Sunny Queen Eggs

Anna Permezel, James Tan, Rod Slater and Kay Cafarella of Cadbury Confectionery

Juliet Van Den Heuval, the Prestige Group

J.D. Millner and Associates, for their Le Creuset range of products

Jan Liddle, Glad Products of Australia

The promotions team at Myer Brisbane City Store

Sally Armonoras, Queensco United Dairy Foods

John Reid, Defiance Milling

John Dart, Trumps Nuts and Dried Fruits

Ian Elliot, CSR, for their range of sugar products

Lois Stocks, author of The Home Confectioner

Designer Trim Pty Ltd, Surry Hills, NSW & Richmond, Vic

Index

Apricot Delights 34

baking tray (sheet) sizes 61
Boiled Sweets (Candies) 40, 42–3
Butterscotch 59

Candied (Crystallised) Fruit 37
Caramels 46
Chocolate Fudge 8
Chocolate Marzipan 14
Coconut Ice 14
Coconut Kisses 21

egg weights 61
English Toffee 45

Fondant 9–10

gas marks 62

hard sweets 38–60
    Boiled Sweets (Candies) 40, 42–3
    Butterscotch 59
    Caramels 46
    English Toffee 45
    Honeycomb 46
    Lollipops 52
    Peanut Brittle 51
    Praline 56, 58
    Sugar Bells 55
    Toffee Apples 48
Honeycomb 46

important notes 61–2

Lollipops 52

Marshmallow 17

Nougat 22

oven temperatures and gas marks 62

Peanut Brittle 51
Praline 56, 58

Royal Icing 62
Rum Balls 32

soft sweets 7–37
    Apricot Delights 34
    Candied (Crystallised) Fruit 37
    Chocolate Fudge 8
    Chocolate Marzipan 14
    Chocolate Ice 14
    Chocolate Kisses 21
    Fondant 9–10
    Marshmallow 17
    Nougat 22
    Rum Balls 32
    Sugared Jellies 18
    Turkish Delight 31
    Walnut Logs 24, 26
    Walnut Marzipan 27–8
    Walnut Toffee Fudge 13

storage 61
sugar, cooking with 61
Sugar Bells 55
sugar (candy) thermometer 61
Sugared Jellies 18

Toffee Apples 48
Turkish Delight 31

Walnut Logs 24, 26
Walnut Marzipan 27–8
Walnut Toffee Fudge 13